"The Gaza Prison"

"The Gaza Prison"

and Other Poems on Common Humanity,
Apartheid, and Antisemitism

S T KIMBROUGH, JR.

FOREWORD BY
Charles Amjad-Ali

RESOURCE *Publications* • Eugene, Oregon

"THE GAZA PRISON"
And Other Poems on Common Humanity, Apartheid, and Anti-Semitism

Copyright © 2024 S T Kimbrough, Jr. All rights reserved. Except for brief quotations in critical publications or reviews, no part of this book may be reproduced in any manner without prior written permission from the publisher. Write: Permissions, Wipf and Stock Publishers, 199 W. 8th Ave., Suite 3, Eugene, OR 97401.

Resource Publications
An Imprint of Wipf and Stock Publishers
199 W. 8th Ave., Suite 3
Eugene, OR 97401

www.wipfandstock.com

PAPERBACK ISBN: 979-8-3852-1978-0
HARDCOVER ISBN: 979-8-3852-1979-7
EBOOK ISBN: 979-8-3852-1980-3

Contents

Foreword | ix
  Charles Amjad-Ali

Introduction | xix
  S T Kimbrough, Jr.

SECTION 1: *Gaza*
  1. The Gaza Prison | 3
  2. A Gazan Mother's Terror | 4
  3. Daily Life in Gaza, December 2023 | 5
  4. Freedom of Movement | 6
  5. A Tragic Hanukkah 2023 | 7
  6. Inhumane | 8
  7. Another Day in the Israel/Gaza War | 9
  8. New Ethnic Cleansing | 10

SECTION 2: *Revenge*
  9. Revenge | 13
  10. The Star of David's Disgrace | 15
  11. Guilty of War Crimes | 17
  12. Just Anger? | 18
  13. Weapons' Wrath | 19
  14. Drones | 20

Contents

SECTION 3: *History*
    15. History Repeats Itself | 23
    16. History's Lesson | 25
    17. Hitleresque Leadership | 26
    18. The Mask Is Off | 27

SECTION 4: *Holy Land?*
    19. Uttermost Hypocrisy | 31
    20. Israel and Hamas | 32
    21. Holiness or Holocaust? | 33
    22. Reclaim "Holy Land" | 34
    23. A Jerusalem Child | 36

SECTION 5: *Common Humanity*
    24. Our Commonness | 39
    25. Interconnected | 40
    26. A New Year of Hope or of Despair | 41
    27. Never Again #1 | 42
    28. Be Humane | 44
    29. Who Wants to Be a Child? | 45
    30. Respect for Whom? | 46

SECTION 6: *Apartheid and Antisemitism*
    31. Apartheid | 49
    32. Resist Apartheid | 50
    33. The Antisemitic Stigma | 51
    34. Psalm 10:2-3 | 53
    35. A Woman of Samaria | 54
    36. *Persona non grata* | 55
    37. Is Ethnic Cleansing a Defense? | 56

SECTION 7: *Justice*
    38. An Ancient Cry for Justice | 59
    39. Do Not Pervert Justice | 60
    40. Justice, Justice Plead! | 61
    41. Justice, Justice Is the Cry | 62
    42. Equality and Justice for All | 63

Contents

SECTION 8: *Grace*
    43. Never Again #2 | 67
    44. Weaponizing the Bible | 69
    45. Grace | 71
    46. Forgiveness | 72
    47. The Art of Forgiveness | 73
    48. Love One's Enemy! Insane! | 74
    49. Humane | 75
    50. To Conquer | 76

Bibliography | 77
Index of Biblical References | 79

FOREWORD

"We All Stand Witness to Horror: The Gaza Prison and Israeli Genocide."[1]

I am highly honored to write a foreword to another brilliant collection of poetry by S T Kimbrough, entitled *"The Gaza Prison" and Other Poems on Common Humanity, Apartheid, and Antisemitism*. As the title indicates, this volume covers one of the deepest crises that we are facing in our contemporary political and moral history, i.e., the all-encompassing, comprehensive, traumatic, and very violent destruction of life, freedoms, institutions, and property in Palestine. Together these are an unmitigated case of state terrorism and horrific genocidal ethnic cleansing. We are all witness to this genocide as we see it happen in real time in our face, all the arguments and unwillingness to accept it as such notwithstanding.

This crisis is, however, also deeply intertwined with the other major existential dilemma that impinges upon us, namely the dubious future of democracy, democratic norms and institutions, the hard fought rights, regimes, and the general principles of justice, righteousness, and ethical moral life. Each of these elements has taken a long hard history of struggle and fighting against well-established traditions of prejudices, as well as the established order of power, and the claims, sometimes even divinized, of some

---

1. Charles Amjad-Ali, Ph.D., Th.D., The Martin Luther King, Jr., Prof. of Justice and Christian Community (Emeritus); and Director of Islamic Studies (Emeritus) at Luther Seminary, MN; and The Desmond Tutu Prof. of Ecumenical Theology and Social Transformation in Africa (Emeritus) at the University of Western Cape, Cape Town, South Africa. The quotation is from his paper "Anti-Semitism—an Epithet to Shield Israel's Apartheid Practices."

existing oligarchies of power. The combination of these crises, dilemmas, and challenges are jeopardizing the very character of social responsibilities and social contracts that we have evolved through these struggles over the last 300 and more years to establish and normalize.

S T has once again, in his inimitable lyrical form, covered this whole gamut and spectrum through his highly poetic creativity, while also capturing the biblical narrative of social and ethical norms. While the genre is poetic, S T addresses the philosophical and theoretical issues of justice, morality, and righteousness, etc., vis-à-vis issues of land, history, and indeed aesthetics, etc. His poetry is therefore situated at the core intersection of literary and political theory, and he does a great job in making his readers comprehend these philosophical and theoretical issues, both intellectually and emotionally. He has also provided us an insight into the biblical and theological narratives[2] for their foundation in a triune God: one who creates all equally in the very image of God (the *imago dei*),[3] who reconciled the whole creation unto Godself at the cross,[4] and the promise of the empowerment and pouring out of God's spirit on all flesh or creation.[5] Given this trinitarian founda-

---

2. See particularly references to the following biblical passages (poem numbers are in parentheses):
Leviticus 11:44 (#22), 19:18 (#27); Deuteronomy 16:19-20 (#39); Psalms 4:4 (#12), 10:2-3 (#34), 33:5 (#41), 140:12 (#41); Isaiah 1:17 (#21, #34); Jeremiah 22:3 (#38); Micah 6:8 (#38); John 4:4-42 (#35); Ephesians 4:26 (#12); 1 John 4:8 (#43, #44).

3. Genesis 1:26-27: "Then God said, 'Let us make *humankind in our image, according to our likeness;*' . . . So God *created humankind in his image, in the image of God he created them; male and female he created them*" (emphasis added).

4. 2 Corinthians 5:19-20: ". . . in Christ God was reconciling *the world* to himself, not counting *their trespasses* against them, and *entrusting the message of reconciliation to us*. So we are ambassadors for Christ, since God is making his appeal through us" (emphasis added).

5. Acts 2:17-18: "In the last days it will be, God declares, that I will pour out my Spirit *upon all flesh*, and your sons and your daughters shall prophesy, and your young men shall see visions, and your old men shall dream dreams. Even upon my slaves, *both men and women,* in those days I will pour out my Spirit; and they shall prophesy" (emphasis added).

tion of the radical equality and the dignity of all in creation, the all-inclusive reconciling salvation and in the all-pervasive empowerment to proclaim this, any restriction and negation of this equality appears to me to be at least quite sacrilegious, if not downright blasphemous. How can we continue to believe that some people are more a creation of God, or more saved by the cross, or more empowered by the Holy Spirit than others? The corollary is that these "others" are simply not part of this undeserved grace, nor part of common humanity and justice, and therefore cannot be included in the biblical imperative that love for the neighbor be equal to the love of God. If they are not part of common humanity, they cannot be the neighbor. Such exclusion is clearly offensive to the triune God, and God's activities in and for the creation.

> How can it be a God of love
>   would choose some people to abuse,
> while placing others far above
>   all justice; does not this confuse
> the Bible's claim that "God is love,"[6]
>   the nature of almighty God?
> If we cannot partake thereof,
>   then Jews and Christians are a fraud.[7]

Unfortunately, even the best of us fall prey to some form of Orwellian allegory, that while "all animals are equal, . . . some are more equal than others."[8] This is clearly evident in our theology, missiology, philosophy, sociology, and also in our politics and political institutions. It is perhaps most clearly manifest in the case of the UN Security Council, which was theoretically created with the foundation of the equality of all humanity, yet allows veto power only to five permanent member countries—who are thus rather more equal than even the other ten elected members,[9] not to men-

---

6. 1 John 4:8.
7. From the poem #43, "Never Again #2."
8. Cf. George Orwell, *Animal Farm* (1945).
9. The permanent members are China, the United States, France, the United Kingdom, and the Russian Federation, while the other ten members are elected, and so change regularly.

tion the rest of the 193 members of the General Assembly. Ironically the Universal Declaration of Human Rights (UDHR) itself was created in the same year that Orwell published his classical allegorical text, *Animal Farm*.

What, however, is most critical about the series of poems presented in this book, is that S T names and shames all those who continue the sacrilegious violations, inhumanities, destruction of dignity, racist bigotry, and overwhelming prejudice against any people whom they have decided are not part of this egalitarian ontological foundation. The identity of the "others" is based on "us" through "our" respective arrogations of normative pseudo-universalizing principles (metaethical norms). This may be on the grounds of sexual definitions, restrictive and narrow understanding of the divine, religious exclusion, color determinations, the privilege and predestination of God's exclusivity, and the exceptionalism determining who owns, occupies, usurps, or steals somebody's land, labor, culture, and property, etc. The "others" are therefore classified as sub-human, and thus dispensable.

> In Israel, Christians, Muslims find
> they're citizens subclass.
> Their ancestors are the wrong kind;
> they're written off *en masse*.[10]

This is not only a fundamental failure in following Christian ethical imperatives, as I have argued above, it is equally a fundamental violation of the UDHR. Even before enumerating these foundations in the Articles, the UDHR states in the very "Preamble" that "recognition of the *inherent dignity and of the equal and inalienable rights of all members of the human family is the foundation of freedom, justice and peace in the world.*" The UDHR then goes on to state in **Article 1** that, "*All human beings are born free and equal in dignity and rights. They are endowed with reason and conscience and should act towards one another in a spirit of brotherhood,*" and in **Article 2** that, "*Everyone is entitled to all the rights and freedoms set forth in this Declaration, without distinction of any kind, such*

10. See poem #36, "*Persona non grata.*"

as race, colour, sex, language, religion, political or other opinion, national or social origin, property, birth or other status."[11] So where should those carrying out the current genocide of the Palestinians in Gaza stand, and where do the signatories and even the authors of these rights stand in the courts who aid, abet, and support this genocide or are even the ones enabling it? What we are witnessing, and what S T articulates so profoundly here, is the violation of this universal international declaration engendered because Germany, with the clear collaboration of the West, had failed so miserably in upholding these norms already established before their enshrinement in the UDHR.

S T shows equally profoundly how the "Jewish Question/ Problem," which was behind the "Final Jewish Solution," has now morphed into the Palestinian Question/Problem and is now being enacted as a "Final Palestinian Solution." The "Jewish Question" has plagued much of European history, since long before the term itself first emerged in Great Britain around 1750 during the debates vis-à-vis the Jewish Naturalisation Act 1753. The Jewish Question was a clear product of the negative attitude toward the Jews as a people, against the background of the rising political nationalism and new nation-states after the Treaty of Westphalia in 1648. The question resurfaced and was discussed again in France (*la question juive*) after the French Revolution in 1789.

According to Holocaust scholar, Lucy Dawidowicz, "the histories of Jewish emancipation and of European antisemitism are replete with proffered 'solutions to the Jewish question.'"[12] Many serious thinkers dealt with this question, for example, in Germany the theologian philosopher Bruno Bauer's treatise *Die Judenfrage* (The Jewish Question) in 1843, and Karl Marx's response in his 1844 essay *Zur Judenfrage*, (On the Jewish Question)[13] before it be-

11. *Universal Declaration of Human Rights*, United Nations Department of Public Information, NY, https://www.ohchr.org/en/human-rights/universal-declaration/translations/english. Emphasis added.

12. See her *The War Against the Jews, 1933-1945* (New York: Holt, Rinehart and Winston. 1975) pp. xxi–xxiii.

13. Karl Marx. "On the Jewish Question" in *Deutsch-Französische Jahrbücher*. February, 1844.

came a Nazi German trumpet call for a politics of oppression, and genocide of the Jewish people, or as it was articulated *die Endlösung der Judenfrage*—the Final Solution of the Jewish Question. Most of Europe knew about what was happening in Germany at the time, and most of Europe ignored it, turning a blind eye to massive human suffering and the destruction of a people. But equally critically the bankruptcy of the "very moral foundations" that the West had claimed for its superiority was now fully displayed in its wanton denial of what was happening under its very nose. It is clear that various institutions and theological positions were generated in the wake of World War II to take away the stigma of this deep inhumanity; yet the genocide; the *Shoah*, was still not washable from history. These negative aspects were already fully established in the colonial racist genocidal patterns starting with 1492 (Christopher Columbus) and 1497 (Vasco da Gama) as the concept of Enlightenment was emerging in Europe. But these European colonialist actions took place outside Europe's territorial terrain and were therefore justified through the self-aggrandizing myth of the "white man's burden,"[14] and so were functionally invisible to Europeans—the *Shoah*, however, displayed the utter bankruptcies of these high claims of civilizational superiority and their actual worth inside Europe itself.

The question remains, how was it possible that a society which has produced some of the greatest philosophers, Enlightenment itself, rational thinking, leading critical theologians, thinkers, social scientists, musicians, writers, et al., could produce such horror and unrepented massive sinfulness and destruction of humanity and even elect Hitler and the Nazi government that become the author and implementer of the most efficient, massive industrial slaughter of a people? I have argued elsewhere that this had its roots not only

---

14. Cf. Rudyard Kipling's famous poem "White Man's Burden: The United States & the Philippine Islands, 1899," first published in the February 1899 issue of *McClure's Magazine*, and later in *Rudyard Kipling's Verse: Definitive Edition*.

in German cultural structures but also in its theology and even more ashamedly in the very Reformation itself.[15]

Daniel Goldhagen, former associate professor at Harvard, in his famous, *Hitler's Willing Executioners: Ordinary Germans and the Holocaust*[16] lays to rest many myths about the Holocaust, e.g., that the German people were ignorant of the mass killing of Jews; that the killers were all SS men, and that those who slaughtered Jews did so reluctantly. Goldhagen provides conclusive evidence that the extermination of European Jewry engaged the energies and enthusiasm of tens of thousands of ordinary Germans. He takes us into the killing fields where Germans voluntarily hunted Jews like animals, tortured them wantonly, and then posed cheerfully for snapshots with their victims. From mobile killing units, to the camps, to the death marches, Goldhagen shows how ordinary Germans, nurtured in a society where Jews were seen as unalterably evil and dangerous, willingly followed their beliefs to their logical conclusion.[17] I would expand upon this profound insight, to include almost all of Europe, as they all knew of it, if not directly the details.

In the wake of this massive weight of inhumanity, Europe and the West set up institutions to prevent such a thing from ever occurring again, such as the UN, etc. They also, out of an abundance of guilt, established the State of Israel itself. Over the decades since, the *"Judenfrage"* of old has obviously morphed into the *"Palästinensische Frage"* (Palestinian question). Here the ones who were originally the victims and seen as non-people and a "problem/question," for Europe (i.e., the Jews), have now become

---

15. Charles Amjad-Ali, "Prejudice and Its Historical Application: A Radical Hermeneutic of Luther's Treatment of the Turks (Muslims) and the Jews" in Ulrich Duchrow and Craig Nessan, eds., *Radicalizing Reformation Volume 4: Liberation from Violence for Life in Peace*, 105–42.

16. Daniel Jonah Goldhagen, *Hitler's Willing Executioners: Ordinary Germans and the Holocaust*.

17. Daniel J. Goldhagen, *A Moral Reckoning: the Role of the Catholic Church in the Holocaust and its Unfulfilled Duty of Repair*. Goldhagen used Luther's work to argue for the deep-rooted unique "eliminationist" antisemitism of German culture.

the victimizers—practicing the same vile prejudices, rhetoric, and violence, and making another people, the Palestinians, their victims and as a non-people.

> *Persona non grata* are words
> each Palestinian hears.
> Oh my, did I forget the Kurds?
> They've heard these words for years.[18]

Highly ironically the US, the West, and Israel are openly violating every norm, every principle articulated by the UN institutions that they themselves authored and are even classifying these institutions as the enemies of Israel and antisemitic.

Palestinians are not given equal treatment in life or in death. The average ratio of Jews versus Palestinians living in Israel's political chaos and oppression is at least roughly 9 to 1, while the death toll of all the conflicts, *intifadas*, etc., is at least 1:16.[19] This war has surpassed even this horrendous ratio and as of 22nd January 2024 it is around 1400 Israelis to well over 25,000 Palestinians, i.e., 1:20. Each Jewish life taken in these clashes is vociferously claimed to be a tragedy and a gross violation of the sacrosanct rights of the Jews in Israel, while the deaths of Palestinians are immediately hailed as just killings, and thus the right and moral response and fully deserved. Given the huge disparity in the death tolls, it is highly offensive and repugnant to see the ceaseless propaganda of the

---

18. The third stanza of poem #36.

19. According to the United Nations Office for the Coordination of Humanitarian Affairs (OCHA), in "confrontations between Palestinians and Israelis in the context of occupation and conflict" between 2008 and 2023, there have been 408 Israeli fatalities as compared to 6,327 Palestinian fatalities (i.e., 6.1% Israelis and 93.9% Palestinians, which is a ratio of 1:17): cf. https://www.ochaopt.org/data/casualties#. Even according to the very conservative Jewish site, the *Jewish Virtual Library: A Project of AICE (American-Israeli Cooperative Enterprise–1988–2023)*, "Vital Statistics: Total Casualties, Arab-Israeli Conflict (1860–present)," between 1948 and 2021, through many campaigns, wars, intifadas and operations, etc., 14,277 Jews/Israelis and 87,840 Arabs/Palestinians have been killed, i.e., 14% Jews and 86% Palestinians, which is a ratio of 1:16. cf. https://www.jewishvirtuallibrary.org/total-casualties-arab-israeli-conflict.

WE ALL STAND WITNESS TO HORROR

Jewish Israelis as the exclusive victims of continuous violence and terrorism. This propaganda is reflected in all aspects of life in the State of Israel vis-à-vis the Palestinians: ranging from political agitations, the ongoing violative constructions of settler communities, to the flouting of international laws vis-à-vis occupied land after the wars of 1967 and 1973. The USA is equally culpable, and it seems that the USA's foreign policy will always support Israel, irrespective of the gross violations of law and established international treaties, etc. The USA is complicit directly and unequivocally in the apartheid and genocide that is currently taking place in Palestine/Israel. It is not possible for Israel to take the steps it does in global politics without the direct aid (financial, arms, and propaganda) and abetting of the USA, which feeds the internal politics of Israel in its dealings with its Palestinian citizens.

This whole book contains absolute gems for insights, moral grammar, and ethical norms. But I have always been struck by certain concepts that I want to highlight here. One of them of course is *collateral damage*, a deeply offensive and horrendous concept which we must all find simply too appalling to ever use. It is not just Orwellian doublespeak; it is always a reminder of the incredible civilian casualties that all wars cause. But instead of fighting against all wars, we have found a justificational concept in "collateral damage" to rationalize killing noncombatants and violate the most ethical principle that "thou shall not kill." It is ironic that the expression *collateral damage* was generated in the Vietnam war—a most unjust colonial and highly unethical war that was committed by the most powerful nation on the earth over several decades against a much less potent and weaker projected enemy. The expression *collateral damage* has since become entrenched in the US military jargon and through it by all those in power who commit wars. It should be simply taken out and thoroughly challenged. Especially now as there is a parallel claim to have highly sophisticated smart weapons that target the specific persons we want to kill and yet we continue to use the expression *collateral damage* rather than admit that the weapons are not as smart as we claim and that all wars, whatever the ostensible reasoning behind them, entail a very high death toll of noncombatants, and thus fail miserably on the grounds of morality and even the standards established as part of Just War Theory/ies.

This war will continue even when the guns are officially silenced, given the total destruction of all the infra-structure that makes life possible. So in fact more people are likely to die of hunger, malnutrition, total lack of hospitalization, and even educational possibility, than just from the vile and unjust conflict carried out by Israel against the Palestinians. No amount of crocodile tears now will ever take away the deep and bloody stain of our full support of and part in this genocide and ethnic killing. So history will once again demand from the West the confessional *mea culpa, mea culpa, mea maxima culpa* with hope that God in God's mercy does indeed forgive sinners. S T's poems leave us with the robust hope and knowledge of this loving and forgiving God in spite of our horrors, genocides, and ethnic cleansing. Thanks, S T.

> God's grace is all of this and more,
>   encompassing the universe.
> It has unceasing love in store;
>   love can the power of hate reverse.[20]

Charles Amjad-Ali, Ph.D., Th.D.
January 2024

---

20. This is the last stanza of poem #45, "Grace."

Introduction

FOR DECADES PEOPLE HAVE heard the name "Gaza" used in a variety of contexts. It designates the smaller of two Palestinian territories (the other is the West Bank). It is located on the eastern coast of the Mediterranean Sea. On the southwest it is bordered by Egypt and on the east and north by Israel. Also known as the Gaza Strip, it is 25 miles (41 kilometers) long and 3.7 to 7.5 miles (6 to 12 kilometers) wide, depending on the location.

At the time of the 1948 Arab-Israeli war, Gaza came under the control of Egypt and was a refuge for Palestinians who were fleeing or were being expelled during that war. During the 1967 Six-Day War, Gaza was overtaken and occupied by Israel. The result was the subsequent occupation of the Palestinian territories by the State of Israel. The Oslo Accords, established during the 1990s, created the Palestinian Authority (PA) dominated by the Fatah party. It was to have oversight of the West Bank and Gaza. In 2006, however, the Fatah authority over Gaza was replaced by the election of the Hamas organization, a militant Sunni Muslim party.

Though Israel withdrew its military forces from Gaza in 2005, thereafter it established a blockade of Gaza restricting imports by land, air, and sea. Therefore, people and goods could not enter the Gaza territory by these means. This is why Gaza has often been referred to as the largest "open-air prison" in the world.

On October 7, 2023, Hamas attacked an area of southern Israel, resulting in approximately 1400 people killed and many hostages were taken. This occurred on the last day of the Jewish

Introduction

holiday of Sukkot. Israel vowed to destroy Hamas because of this horrific attack. Since the Israeli offensive against and into Gaza ca. 34,000 Palestinians have been killed, the majority being women and children. This is the figure released by the health ministry in Gaza. Much of Gaza is now completely destroyed.

The poems in this book reflect on the horrors of war and the unjust effects of decades of occupation of Palestinian territory by Israel.

Section 1 is titled simply *Gaza* and reflects on the life of imprisonment there, a life that results in the difficulty of procuring food, electricity, health care, and heat in winter months. While it is often easy to describe situations such as these in generalities, a realistic glimpse is expressed in "A Gazan Mother's Terror."

> Her life is difficult enough:
>   no water or electric pow'r,
> her children's hunger, no foodstuff,
>   their situation is most dour.
> The Red Cross tried, could not get through
>   to help her neighbor's dying son.
> There were no options to pursue;
>   there was no help from anyone. (#2)[1]

The one-percent Christian population in Gaza without aid from Israel, has often found itself aided by fellow Palestinians regardless of creed. In "Daily Life in Gaza, December 2023" one reads of a destitute Gazan Christian family in despair, having lost everything.

> Just then their former neighbors came,
>   right after Friday prayers,
> and spoke to each of them by name:
>   "We're all caught unawares!
> A tank is coming down the street,
>   destroying all in sight."
> Their fear was felt with each heartbeat;
>   all that was left was fright.

---

1. Following all excerpts from poems in this volume that are quoted in the Introduction the number of the poem will appear within parentheses, e.g. (#2).

Introduction

> Behind a shattered mosque they'd found
>   a giant, bombed-out hole
> that led far down into the ground,
>   where they saw not a soul.
> The father of their neighbors said,
>   "Come quickly, follow me,
> I've found a tunnel which has led
>   to a safe place, you'll see." (#3)

Confined to Gaza, the Palestinians living there can go nowhere, except as possibly they are permitted release for some specific work in Israel. There is absolutely no "Freedom of Movement."

> The Gaza Palestinians are
>   to boundaries confined
> by Israel's laws that are bizarre—
>   to justice they are blind. (#4)

Section 2, "Revenge," addresses the matters of revenge on the part of Israel's and Hamas's responses. In spite of trying to explain away the motives of revenge in Hamas attacks on Israel and Israel's attacks on Gaza, there are too many examples of statements and acts of revenge to smooth over evil intentions. Will human beings never learn from history that fighting revenge with revenge and hate with hate eventually leads to self-destruction?

> The war's revenge is filled with hate:
>   cleanse Hamas' hatred with revenge,
> cleanse hate with hate, lest it's too late,
>   a concept older than Stonehenge. (#6)

One may seek to confine revenge, so that in this case, the goal is specifically to destroy just the leadership of Hamas. However, the collateral damage far outweighs the so-called specificity of this goal. Thousands of innocent women and children have been thoughtlessly killed.

> Revenge in Israel today
>   by Palestinian or Jew
> supports the goal, thousands to slay
>   and never, never just a few.

Introduction

> . . .
> Revenge leads only to despair
>   for the avenger and avenged,
>   for vengeance is a sad affair,
>   which will leave both of them unhinged. (#9)

Can you imagine the desecration of the sacred symbol, the Star of David, by burning it on the face of a Palestinian by Israeli policemen? In a few minutes they turn a sacred symbol into a symbol of hatred, and thereby they denigrate the Jewish faith and its traditions.

> The sacred star they weaponize
>   to do an awful, evil deed.
> And little do they recognize
>   that peace forever they impede.
>
> The Star of David thus means hate,
>   that life disfigures with intent,
> intent: the faith of Jews berate
>   and in the name of Jews torment. (#10)

Section 3, "History," addresses the repetition of history as regards war. It is particularly disheartening that in a place such as the Holy Land with its rich and tragic history, modern day Israel and Hamas have learned little or nothing from history. Humankind's inhumane action is a spiral of repetition through the ages, and once again it occurs in the land called "Holy." In addition to Hamas' October 7, 2023, attack in Israel, and Israel's subsequent attacks in Gaza, one finds Israeli settlers wearing paramilitary uniforms and bearing weapons while attacking Palestinians on their properties in the West Bank, hoping to run them out.

> Yes, history repeats, repeats:
>   what Nazis did to Jews,
> in Israel in towns, on streets
>   a Nazi spirit brews.
> . . .

INTRODUCTION

> Yet, there is good in history,
>   why not the good repeat?
> Make goodness not a mystery,
>   instead a daily feat. (#15)

Democracy, as noble an attempt as it is, will die if it succumbs to Hitleresque Leadership and activity. In addition, the attempts to rewrite the history of the region known as the Holy Land that portray Jews, before the founding of the State of Israel, as the victims of injustices perpetrated by the Palestinians, who usurped a land that was not theirs, are ludicrous.

> They rewrite hist'ry, victims play
>   as though divine right of past kings
> were theirs to claim each day on day,
>   while rights of others all take wings!
>
> The mask of "made-up" history
>   the state of Israel gladly wears.
> But hist'ry's truth it can't conceal,
>   truth will expose Israel's affairs! (#18)

Section 4 bears the title "Holy Land?" The question mark is not a mistake. Perhaps the poems in this section may help us question why we call a land "holy" that is filled with so much violence and hate. Three major world religions, Judaism, Christianity, and Islam, regard many places in Palestine and neighboring countries as sacred to their faith traditions. And yet in this land—

> Oppressor and oppressed maim, kill
> men, women, children at their will. (#20)

These are daily occurrences in the "Holy Land."

> In Zion, Scripture's Holy Hill,
>   looms a new Holocaust,
> and Palestinians, Jews now kill,
>   no matter what the cost.
> Then there's Israeli payback,
>   now measured in lives killed,
> for Hamas' terrible attack,
>   revenge must be fulfilled.

Introduction

. . .

> One cannot "Holy Land" reclaim
> with Nazi *savoir faire*.
> What an insult to every name
> of saints who have lived there. (#22)

Section 5 is titled "Common Humanity," which seeks to beckon the clashing forces of the Holy Land, in spite of creedal, faith, and political differences, to recognize their common humanity. Our bodies, regardless of ethnicity, race, or religion, all breathe in oxygen in order to stay alive. This we all have in common.

> Though faiths and cultures aren't the same,
> the breath of life we breathe
> should never anger, hate inflame,
> make us with hatred seethe.
>
> The breath we breathe keeps us alive;
> the function is the same.
> Let us then find the ways to thrive
> all humankind can claim. (#24)

Is there no commonness Jews, Christians, and Muslims can find by which they can live in peace?

> The books of Christians, Muslims, Jews
> all emphasize a neighbor love
> but what we read in modern news,
> says some place self-love far above. (#27)

In the current Israel/Hamas war, it has been said by high officials, "This is no time for love, no time for forgiveness."

> "No time for love," many now say,
> "It's time to show we won't retreat.
> The time is ours, out of our way!
> You'll never us and ours defeat."
> Who will revive God's neighbor love,
> which in the Bible has its place?
> It pleads, let nothing rise above
> a neighbor love in every race! (#27)

INTRODUCTION

Section 6 treats two very difficult but timely subjects: apartheid and antisemitism. In Israel apartheid is practiced as segregation of Palestinians, who are non-Jews. Palestinians in Israel, even those "legitimately" allowed to live in the current State of Israel, are second-class citizens, though the term "citizens" must be loosely applied here. Palestinians in the West Bank and in East Jerusalem have been pushed out of their homes, denied access to legitimately owned farms and other properties. And sometimes they have even been put in jail for refusing to move off their land.

> "Apartheid" now we hear again,
> for Israel inflicts the pain
> on Palestinians day by day,
> and ethnic cleansing has its way.
> Why does the world not hear the cry
> as Palestinians daily die?
> Like blacks, browns in South Africa
> and slaves brought to America,
> the Palestinians suffer wrong.
> They too now ask, "How long? How long?" (#31)

How different is this from the practice of apartheid in South Africa? And in many ways how different from the practice of the Nazis against the Jews? Perhaps it has been a slower process in Israel, but the similarities are frightening.

The rights that Palestinians have in Israel are to die and to be objects of hate and ridicule.

> The Palestinians are the ones
> that Israel wants to rout.
> With bombs and automatic guns,
> it wants to get them out. (#32)

When one criticizes this form of prejudice, the term "antisemitic" is used by some who hope to stigmatize those who offer critique of a cruel and prejudicial apartheid system.

> The Nazis practiced genocide
> and confiscated homes and goods.
> Injustices they amplified—
> destroying Jewish neighborhoods.

Introduction

> Ironically Israel now
>   repeats this horrid history.
> It does so with Nazi know-how
>   through Palestinian misery.
> It confiscates, destroys, and kills
>   the Palestinian populus;
> imprisons them as it so wills.
>   Its actions are unscrupulous. (#33)

Is it then antisemitic to criticize and oppose such immoral behavior when it is practiced in Israel?

I wonder, is the following a common perspective shared by Judaism, Christianity, and Islam?

> Samaritan, gentile, or Jew,
>   we drink from the same well.
> God's living love springs forth for you,
>   for all who on earth dwell. (#35)

Section 7 bears the title "Justice." Strange it is that in a land where Hebrew prophets pled for justice for all, that this word and its practice today are not simply subdued, rather they have vanished as regards the relationship between Israelis and Palestinians.

> The prophet Amos pleads and pleads:
>   let justice rush like streams[2]
> of living water, meeting needs
>   of those with justice dreams.
>
> Isaiah says, "Learn to do good,
>   seek justice for th'oppressed."[3]
> And Jeremiah says you should
>   "Seek justice, you'll be blessed."[4]

. . .

---

2. Amos 5:24.
3. Isaiah 1:17.
4. Jeremiah 22:3.

INTRODUCTION

> Yes, justice, justice is the theme
>   of Hebrew prophets' speech.
> Who's willing this cause to redeem?
>   Is it beyond all reach? (#38)

Today it is as though the voice of the Hebrew prophets few in Israel choose to hear. Nevertheless, some like to say that, according to biblical prophecy, God has bequeathed the land of Palestine to modern-day Jews. This is the way they weaponize the Hebrew Scriptures, at least one feature of it, while completely ignoring the ancient cry for justice which they smother so that it will not be heard.

> Apartheid and segregation,
>   are basically the same.
> The new name a "Jewish Nation"
>   excludes non-Jews by name,
> especially Palestinians—
>   no human rights, no land.
> Whatever your opinions,
>   for justice take a stand! (#42)

Section 8 titled "Grace" is the concluding section of the book and raises questions regarding the possibilities of grace in the present and future of Israel and Palestine. To those who believe that the "land of Israel" is a sole divine gift to Jews based on their views of the Hebrew Scriptures, the time has come to ask some serious questions.

> The colonializing voices cry,
>   consistently, "That's mine, that's mine!"
> It matters not who'll have to die:
>   the victor's rights are rights divine.
> Today some Christians and some Jews
>   avow, God promised Jews the land.
> In Palestine God will suffuse
>   the chosen people, as God planned.

Introduction

> How can it be a God of love
> would choose some people to abuse,
> while placing others far above
> all justice? Does not this confuse
> the Bible's claim that God is love,[5]
> the nature of almighty God?
> If we cannot partake thereof,
> then Jews and Christians are a fraud. (#43)

There are also other questions we must ask at this time of discord and war. Where can grace be found amid all the turmoil of war? Is there such a thing as free and unmerited goodwill of people toward one another, as one often speaks of the free and unmerited favor of God to all people? Is there a place in the world for courteous goodwill?

> Is grace something that one can learn?
> Is grace something that can be taught?
> Can grace be found where'er you turn?
> Is grace something that's better caught?
>
> You do not know if you have grace,
> but grace is something you can give.
> You'll find that grace will leave a trace,
> and grace is the best way to live.
> . . .
>
> God's grace is all of this and more,
> encompassing the universe.
> It has unceasing love in store;
> love can the power of hate reverse. (#45)

One way that grace is caught is to forgive. But we are told by some Israeli officials that this is not a time to forgive or forget. This is tragic indeed. There will never be healing without forgiveness.

> Forgiveness is not a born trait;
> for many it comes much too late,
> yet it can overcome one's hate. (#46)

---

5. 1 John 4:8.

Introduction

In the current war many feel that the words of a Palestinian Jew named Jesus, "Love your enemies and pray for those who persecute you" (Matthew 5:44), are absolutely ludicrous.

> Some scoff at Jesus' simple way
> to care for others, come what may.
> "To love an enemy's insane,"
> say those who Jesus' way disdain.
> To those who simply can't decide
> the world awaits this to be tried. (#48)

SECTION 1
Gaza

1. The Gaza Prison

The largest prison on the earth,
the State of Israel's given birth.
It's known well as the Gaza Strip,
a land o'erwhelmed by censorship!
One hundred forty-one square miles
is Gaza, where one rarely smiles.
A major part of Palestine,
now Gaza's Israel's prison shrine.
The Gazans have lost all their rights,
injustice taken to new heights.
No passports, there's nowhere to go;
no ships may dock, Israel says so.
No commerce takes place in or out.
The Gazans stripped of dignity
are desperate humanity.
While Israel maintains a blockade,
the Gazans can but plead for aid.
No airport means no aid by air,
a truly inhumane affair.
Dehumanizing atmosphere,
the Gazans daily live in fear.
A child is shot along a street
by soldiers who may this repeat.
The Gazan children live in fear,
each day, each night, each year on year.
The largest prison on the earth
the State of Israel's given birth.

2. A Gazan Mother's Terror

Now waiting for a single hour
    of respite from the missile blasts,
a mother and her children cower
    not knowing how long terror lasts.
Her house was once a place of peace,
    since both her children were born there,
but down the street her nephew, niece
    fled with their parents in despair.

Now Israel's army is so close
    a Gazan mother's terrified.
The angry acts of war are gross;
    all human rights are set aside.
The bombs strike hospitals and shops
    and take life indiscriminately.
The gunfire never, never stops;
    it strikes and kills deliberately!

Her life is difficult enough:
    no water or electric pow'r,
her children's hunger, no foodstuff,
    their situation is most dour.
The Red Cross tried, could not get through
    to help her neighbor's dying son.
There were no options to pursue;
    there was no help from anyone.

3. Daily Life in Gaza, December 2023

A single Christian family
    in Gaza City's left.
They're struggling in grave misery,
    and now are found bereft,
bereft of dwelling and of food,
    bereft of hope at all.
The sense of terror's not subdued,
    because of death's close call.

Just then their former neighbors came,
    right after Friday prayers,
and spoke to each of them by name:
    "We're all caught unawares!
A tank is coming down the street
    destroying all in sight."
Their fear was felt with each heartbeat;
    all that was left was fright.

Behind a shattered mosque they'd found
    a giant, bombed-out hole
that led far down into the ground,
    where they saw not a soul.
The father of their neighbors said,
    "Come quickly, follow me,
I've found a tunnel which has led
    to a safe place, you'll see."

"You'll have to hold another's hands,
    we have no lights to see."
Then suddenly a voice cried out,
    "Come quickly, carefully."
They saw a light and followed on;
    and there these longtime friends
held hands so tightly till the dawn—
    life should lead to such ends.

4. Freedom of Movement

Wherever I may go today,
    one fact is crystal clear:
some folk aren't free to go their way
    to places far and near.

The Gaza Palestinians are
    to boundaries confined
by Israel's laws that are bizarre—
    to justice they are blind.

They have no rights to travel far,
    and no rights to free trade,
and freedom's merely a memoir
    for which for years they've prayed.

The entire world should also pray
    that Gazans may be free,
for Israel's laws justice betray.
    This is quite plain to see!

5. A Tragic Hanukkah 2023

For Hanukkah, let's celebrate
    the victory over Gazans?
The women, children that we hate;
    are they as strong as Tarzans?
The thousands of them that we've killed,
    America, you should be proud.
Don't stop until all Gaza's stilled,
    each Gazan life wrapped in a shroud.

Oh, Hanukkah, time of great joy,
    a time to welcome old and new,
the State of lsrael will destroy
    your meaning that all hold in view.
For now you practice genocide
    of Gazan Palestinians,
whom you for years have occupied
    as part of your dominions.

While Hanukkah recalls the time
    of ancient Israelites' defeat
of violence, unjust rules, and crime,
    a wicked ruler to unseat,
now Hanukkah means sadness, grief;
    its joy now Israel takes away.
Can genocide strengthen belief—
    innocent lives that soldiers slay?

The violence of Hamas decry—
    with violence more lives they take—
some folks do not survive, they die,
    and hostages of some they make.
To kill and capture, history tells
    will lead to more, more of the same,
and casts some lasting, morbid spells
    of greed and hate to kill and maim.

6. Inhumane

This Christmas[1] Israel wages war;
    it claims that it's against Hamas,
but Gazan families near and far
    experience horrific loss.

Schools, hospitals bombed recklessly
    deprives the future of young minds,
while patients suffer endlessly.
    Despair, despair is all one finds.

The war's revenge is filled with hate:
    cleanse Hamas' hatred with revenge,
cleanse hate with hate, lest it's too late,
    a concept older than Stonehenge.

When humans act so inhumane
    and others would annihilate,
their actions are inane, insane;
    for humanness they abdicate.

---

1. 2023.

7. Another Day in the Israel/Gaza War

Under her feet was broken glass
    from windows of her room.
Though carefully she tried to pass
    to reach her mother's broom,
the shattered pieces cut her feet,
    her shoes torn by the blast,
that rocked each house along the street.
    How long would the pain last?

Each step she took was marked by blood,
    each step by hideous pain.
She screamed and noticed where she stood—
    the floor filled with blood stain.
Her father heard her anguished cry
    and caught her as she fell.
He cried, "Who can war dignify?
    The horrors of this hell?"

He gently took his daughter's feet
    into his trembling hands,
removed glass pieces quite petite;
    each foot wrapped with cloth bands.
He held her in his fond embrace
    and calmed her frenzied cry.
Yes, even in war we find a trace
    of love's enduring why.

8. New Ethnic Cleansing

New ethnic cleansing is in vogue!
    In Israel it thrives again,
for Israel now plays the rogue
    and drives out Gazans for its gain.

America supplies the cash
    for Israel to drive them out,
to treat the Gazans all as trash:
    It's ethnic cleansing, there's no doubt!

"Let's drive Hamas into the ground!"
    is Israel's alarming cry,
"And kill all others till they're found;
    there's no excuse, Gazans must die!"

SECTION 2

Revenge

9. Revenge

Revenge can take on many forms:
    for some it seems a civil right,
for others it means constant storms
    against opposing views, a fight.

Revenge does not mean reconcile;
    revenge means to oppose, oppose.
Revenge means others to defile,
    their thoughts and actions to depose.

It often means obliterate;
    perhaps it means annihilate.
Revenge does not commensurate,
    for usually it's controlled by hate.

Revenge inflicts more pain on pain,
    perhaps to hurt and harm someone.
Revenge may a solution fain,
    but seeks to see that harm is done.

Revenge in Israel today
    by Palestinian or Jew
supports the goal, thousands to slay
    and never, never just a few.

Now Israel has the upper hand
    with weapon stores of missiles, tanks,
and vast control of all the land.
    While Gazans die, should Jews give thanks?

Revenge does not seek to be just,
    for justice it has no concern.
It has one goal: fulfill the lust
    to see opponents burn and burn.

Revenge leads only to despair
    for the avenger and avenged,
for vengeance is a sad affair,
    which will leave both of them unhinged.

Avner Gvaryahu (a former Israeli soldier who is the current executive director of the Israeli-based non-profit "Breaking the Silence" that opposes many of Israel's policies) posted:

"Israeli Policemen beat up a Palestinian resident of Shuafat refugee camp, covered his face, tied him up, punched him and seared a Star of David on his face. 16 police officers with 16 body cams—all malfunctioned. One Palestinian with a tattooed Star of David."

I feel sick pic.twitter.com,e/birBqorEtc

The posting also included a photo of the man's branded face with the Star of David on it. How horrific, how inhumane!

10. The Star of David's Disgrace

The blasphemous policemen's act
    to brand upon a young man's face
a Star of David, a sick act,
    which all Israelis will disgrace.

Upon a Palestinian's face
    a sacred symbol is blasphemed.
This evil act one can't erase—
    how Israel's policemen schemed,

they schemed through prejudice and hate
    this sacred symbol to disown—
the Jewish faith to denigrate,
    as if Jews God had never known.

The sacred star they weaponize
    to do an awful, evil deed.
And little do they recognize
    that peace forever they impede.

The Star of David thus means hate
    that life disfigures with intent,
intent: the faith of Jews berate
    and in the name of Jews torment.

11. Guilty of War Crimes

The evil Israel perpetrates
    and calls "defense" exceeds
all hope, and cease-fire talks stalemates
    to stop inhuman deeds
of killing Christians at a church,
    a daughter and her mom,
while other Gazans start a search
    after a loud car-bomb.

It's ethnic cleansing by the Jews
    of Muslims, Christians too.
How strange that Israel shares the views
    of Hitler's motley crew,
who sought a gruesome solution:
    "Rid Germany of Jews,"
a "final, final solution,"
    which Israel now renews.

Wipe out each Palestinian,
    called, "worthless human trash,"
and share the bold opinion:
    "We'll turn their homes to ash."
But hist'ry will surely judge you
    as guilty of war crimes.
Who can be proud to be a Jew
    in these horrific times?

Psalms 4:4, "When you are angry[2] and do not sin; ponder it on your beds, and be silent."

Ephesians 4:26, "Be angry and do not sin; do not let the sun go down on your anger."

12. Just Anger?

Just anger with a moral core
    despises unjust acts and deeds:
deception, lying, stealing, more
    that from distorted minds proceeds.

But anger without moral sense,
    that's aimed at other folk with rage,
destroys the self at great expense,
    if anger one cannot assuage.

All anger that is uncontrolled
    can lead to violence, ev'n death,
as if to Satan one has sold
    like Faust his soul and his last breath.

---

2. NRSV reads "disturbed."

13. Weapons' Wrath

The inhumanity of war
    with weapons minus all respect
for life—they're lethal to the core;
    their goal is simply death's effect.

Whether the cause is just or wrong,
    all weapons are not ethical.
They only demonstrate they're strong;
    their strength is not aesthetical.

Their goal is simply to destroy
    all structures, beings in their path.
And when they fail, they redeploy
    to vent on all their weapons' wrath.

14. Drones

One hears the drones of honey bees,
but there are other drones one sees,
the drones that now are used in war.
One knows exactly what they're for.
They are a guidance system's guide,
overt attacks to lead and hide.
I'd rather hear the drones of bees.
than hear the drones of drones one sees.

SECTION 3
History

15. History Repeats Itself

Yes, history repeats, repeats
    in many frightening ways.
The Germans endured two defeats,
    aggression never pays.

Within one century they waged
    two wars that were worldwide.
They ended with a world outraged
    and hatred amplified.

In Yemen, Ukraine, Palestine—
    the wars rage on and on.
The greedy cry resounds, "That's mine!"
    And hatred's not withdrawn.

In Yemen, Israel, Ukraine,
    though there are cries for peace,
some leaders simply peace disdain,
    and warlords poor folk fleece.

Yes, history repeats, repeats:
    what Nazis did to Jews,
in Israel's towns and on its streets
    a Nazi spirit brews.

There Palestinian homes are razed,
    are ravaged and destroyed.
Like *Kristalnacht*[3] this action's praised,
    as Nazi power's employed.

---

3. "Night of the Broken Glass" was a pogrom against the Jews by the Nazis in Germany on November 9–10, 1938.

Yet there is good in history,
    why not the good repeat?
Make goodness not a mystery,
    instead a daily feat.

16. History's Lesson

In reading history you'll find
    that it repeats again
with good and evil intertwined;
    in one unending chain.

A child is born and hopes arise,
    who will the newborn be?
Will its vocation all surprise,
    remain a mystery?

Will she be wealthy or be poor,
    be of bright intellect?
At birth one never can be sure
    or know what to expect.

From history we're quick to learn
    some grow and seek the good,
while others goodness, kindness spurn,
    some don't act as they should.

That good and evil both are here
    on planet earth, we know.
We struggle with them every year,
    some keep them in escrow.

We cannot balance good and hate,
    or balance war and peace.
For hist'ry shows our tragic state:
    that war and hate don't cease.

Each generation has the chance
    to stand for dignity,
for only this can peace advance,
    make hate futility.

17. Hitleresque Leadership

The menace of mean-willed leadership
in governmental and civil discourse
has no thought of others' needs,
serves itself alone, and demands
that others see things its way.
This is a Nazi perspective
that disregards all other views.
It turns all opposition into hate.
It radicalizes the simplest thoughts.
Beware: see things in one sole way,
a Hitleresque bold view:
agree with me or you are finished.
Agree only with this view, only it!
There is no other option. None!
Agree, dare not to disagree,
for disagreement carries cost,
the cost not only of your rights,
the cost eventually of your life.
Though Naziism was once defeated,
it seeks to rise and rise again.
It allows no freedom of thought,
and opposes all opposition forever!
America was not born for this,
even with its racism and injustice.
Democracy, noble though it be,
will die under Hitleresque leadership.

18. The Mask Is Off

The mask is off, who put it on
    to shield the truth of prejudice?
The Holy Land is now forlorn
    and stands upon a precipice,

the precipice of lies and hate.
    Though saints and prophets both held high
the truth, it's drowned in gross deceit,
    for Israel's leaders truth decry.

They rewrite hist'ry, victims play
    as though divine right of past kings
were theirs to claim each day on day,
    while rights of others all take wings!

The mask of "made-up" history
    the state of Israel gladly wears.
But hist'ry's truth it can't conceal,
    truth will expose Israel's affairs!

Affairs of evil and of good,
    historians will expose them all.
So, Israel, it's time you should
    seek justice quickly, lest you fall.

SECTION 4
Holy Land?

19. Uttermost Hypocrisy

The Palestinians in Jenin[4]
now live through times they've never seen.
With confiscated homes and lands,
a people with which Israel brands
as "not a people but a scourge."
This gives the youth today the urge
to stand up strongly and resist
the claim on which some Jews insist:
"You have no right to life and land,
from this time on you will be banned."
Devoid of human dignity,
now Israel promotes bigotry.
"Jenin's inhabitants let die,"
A viewpoint Israel won't deny.
To call Israel democracy
is uttermost hypocrisy!

---

4. Jenin is a Palestinian city in the occupied West Bank. It once had a population of ca. 50,000, but now has a large refugee camp housing Palestinians who were expelled or fled their homes in the 1948 Palestine War.

20. Israel and Hamas

Oppressor and oppressed maim, kill
men, women, children at their will.
Oppressors have the upper hand.
Will anyone be left to stand?
Which side has latest weaponry
that wipes out life effectively?
Oppressors have the latest skill
and nuclear weapons that will kill.
Can no one cry, "Be human, stop!
instead of blasting each rooftop?"
The inhumanity of war
brings one to ask, "What is life for?"—
to murder and possess the land,
no opposition left to stand?
How can the poor of Palestine
to poverty and death resign,
and in the place called "Holy Land"
where holiness seems to be banned?

21. Holiness or Holocaust?

Keep the Gazans desperate, poor
    with constant-failed economy;
and never let them feel secure
    by land, by air, or by the sea.

Make them a lasting sacrifice;
    for deeds of Hamas make them pay:
each woman, child, the highest price,
    let them not see another day.

The oil-rich fields under the sea,
    that lie just off the Gazan coast,
claim them as Israel's property,
    so oil-rich Israel can boast.

Do not return evil with good,
    ignore all humane qualities.
No, never do the good you should,
    treat Gazans as your enemies.

Now Holy Land's a Holocaust
    of Palestinian flesh and blood,
and holiness is all but lost:
    the sacred words. "Do justice, good."[5]

5. Isaiah 1:17.

22. Reclaim "Holy Land"

They sing a song of Israel?
    They sing of Palestine?
The latter's done with vitriol.
    This passion they opine.
Just show the flag, the worst of crimes,
    arrested you will be.
In this, the horrid, worst of times,
    do this, you'll not be free.

In Zion, Scripture's Holy Hill,
    looms a new Holocaust,
and Palestinians, Jews now kill,
    no matter what the cost.
Then there's Israeli payback,
    now measured in lives killed.
For Hamas' terrible attack,
    revenge must be fulfilled.

Fulfilled with hate, severe revenge:
    kill Gazans one by one.
Blow every house door off its hinge,
    kill every daughter, son.
Cleanse Gaza of this ethnic curse,
    this Palestinian scourge.
For Zionists there's nothing worse—
    extinction Zionists urge.

For people in the "Holy Land,"
    no matter who they be,
can they not "holy" understand
    and live unselfishly?
The Christians, Muslims, and the Jews,
    who gave the land this name,
should spread across the world the news:
    "We HOLY now reclaim."

One cannot "Holy Land" reclaim
    with Nazi *savoir faire*.
What insult it is to each name
    of saints who have lived there.
"You shall be holy,"[6] says the Lord.
    Exceptions? No, not one.
You'll show compassion, kindness toward
    each parent, daughter, son.

---

6. Leviticus 11:44.

23. A Jerusalem Child

A child born in Jerusalem,
    a Muslim, Christian, or a Jew,
is born unknown into mayhem,
    but sadly this is nothing new.

Why followers of these faiths must hate
    remains a lasting puzzlement.
Must this be all new infants' fate,
    a tragic crime, embezzlement,

embezzlement of their own lives:
    it takes the hope of life away.
A wonder that a child survives,
    when hate and prejudice have sway.

One nation now's for Jews alone,
    where Christians, Muslims once had land.
And Palestinians, hist'ry's shown,
    are doomed if they should take a stand.

A Palestinian Holocaust
    the State of Israel now makes:
takes lives and lands at any cost.
    It is entitled, so it takes.

SECTION 5

Common Humanity

24. Our Commonness

What shall we say of children born,
    one culture to the next?
Their births we praise, their deaths we mourn.
    Why must life be perplexed?

When will we learn their lives to praise
    and live in harmony?
Their lives to honor all their days,
    though we may disagree?

Though faiths and cultures aren't the same,
    the breath of life we breathe
should never anger, hate inflame,
    make us with hatred seethe.

The breath we breathe keeps us alive;
    the function is the same.
Let us then find the ways to thrive
    all humankind can claim.

25. Interconnected

Interconnected though we are,
    as humans all are born,
this has not brought us very far,
    which gives us cause to mourn.

Yes, humans all of us may be;
    we're mammals who can think,
but violence, our reality,
    transpires in an eye-blink.

Since humans occupy the earth,
    with war they play the fool,
and think to take another's worth
    by war; it's their best tool.

The world of science makes us wise
    to live in better ways.
Will we this wisdom then despise,
    as every war displays?

If humans are born to connect
    from birth until the grave,
will we connection then reject:
    to wars remain a slave?

Interconnected we can be
    by power we possess:
the heart of connectivity
    is love that all can bless.

26. A New Year of Hope or of Despair

    Again here comes another year
    which gives so many cause for cheer.
They're thankful life has been so kind
    to give them pause to celebrate
    and love to others activate;
to show it's always on their mind.
    No matter faith, or race, or creed,
    inclusive love they know they need.

    But as we face another year
    there're those who daily live in fear.
They don't have shelter, don't have food.
    Their children suffer day and night
    enduring a most desperate plight.
The plea for peace just does no good.
    They have the ever-nagging thought
    that they must live and die for naught.

    Perhaps war's left them destitute
    with enemies who're resolute
to wipe out all their families.
    Amazing in this century
    to find there is such treachery,
such obvious brutalities.
    Hamas and Israel both know
    they're guilty of this dreadful show.

27. Never Again #1

Israelis, Palestinians
    are both born in God's earthly realm.
Regardless of opinions,
    must one the other overwhelm?
The books of Christians, Muslims, Jews
    all emphasize a neighbor love
but what we read in modern news,
    says some place self-love far above.

Above this social principle
    are claims now of the chosen few
who think they are invincible;
    they think God's told them what to do.
The chosen few now take the land
    of aliens, strangers living there;
it's thus they Palestinians brand,
    a tragic, dastardly affair.

Thus neighbor love has not a chance,
    revenge and vengeance take its place,
and life is ruled then by the lance,
    for neighbor love there is no space.
How can the chosen few believe
    that God endorses theft and war?
This is a god that they conceive
    non-chosen people will ignore.

The wars of humankind in time
    relate the bleakest history:
Where is the justice, where's the crime?
    We languish in our misery.
Do we believe earth is God's realm
    created for all human good?
Do we believe God's at the helm
    in Israel, each neighborhood?

"No time for love," many now say,
    "It's time to show we won't retreat.
The time is ours, out of our way!
    You'll never, us and ours defeat."
Who will revive God's neighbor love,
    which in the Bible[7] has its place?
It pleads, let nothing rise above
    a neighbor love in every race!

---

7. Leviticus 19:18, "You shall love your neighbor as yourself."

28. Be Humane

To be humane is no small task,
to be humane you cannot mask
sincerity and genuine care
with nonchalance and a blank stare.

To be humane you need a heart
that's open, caring from the start
of life until it ends in night,
for caring is your own birthright.

You look and listen carefully
with utmost sensitivity.
Compassion and benevolence,
civility without defense

of biases and one's own view
are qualities that you'll accrue.
Who'll be humane in politics,
diplomacy without new tricks?

Who'll be humane and stop all wars,
stop acting like the dinosaurs
that now are totally extinct?
Will humans with such fate be linked?

29. Who Wants to Be a Child?

A child can't choose where it is born,
    in Russia, China, USA,
in towns along the Matterhorn,
    for this is just the human way.

A child is born without a thought
    of being Muslim, Christian, Jew,
for prejudices must be taught;
    the chances for free thought are few.

But every child's born with the right
    to breathe, be nourished, and be free,
Yet some will only know the fright
    of hatred and of poverty.

It's time all children had the choice
    to think, to learn, and to be free,
and without fear to lift their voice
    for justice and for liberty.

But it's the Muslims, Christians, Jews,
    and other faith protagonists,
who daily propagate the news:
    We are the chief antagonists.

Of children Jesus plainly said,
    to them belongs the heavenly realm.
Yet on this earth they've suffered, bled.
    It's fair to ask, Who's at the helm?"

30. Respect for Whom?

The western plains are open wide
    where native tribes once dwelled,
extending to the Great Divide,
    where Rocky Mountains swelled.

The Indian wars, the Trail of Tears,
    diminished native tribes,
left remnants here and there with fears
    from treaties, empty bribes.

Deceived they were at every turn
    and driven from their lands.
In Oklahoma you can learn
    of some surviving bands.

With thirty million natives dead,
    caused by invading whites.
A native child lived with a dread,
    a fear which reached new heights.

This kind of ethnic cleansing's still
    alive in Palestine.
One asks, Why is there yet no will
    such hatred to malign?

It is alive elsewhere on earth,
    where humans never learn,
that every human, every birth,
    respect need never earn.

Respect remains the lone birthright
    of every human soul.
But why then must some for it fight?
    Respect makes humans whole.

SECTION 6
Apartheid and Antisemitism

31. Apartheid

"Apartheid," the world loudly cried;
South Africa, nowhere to hide.
The people there rose to the cry,
and heard the stories how they die
from malice, injustice, and hate;
apartheid these could not abate.
How whites decried the life of blacks,
suppressed them, kept them on their backs.
"Apartheid" now we hear again,
for Israel inflicts the pain
on Palestinians day by day,
and ethnic cleansing has its way.
Why does the world not hear the cry
as Palestinians daily die?
Like blacks, browns in South Africa
and slaves brought to America,
the Palestinians suffer wrong.
They too now ask, "How long? How long?"
Deprived of freedom, rights to work,
Israelis daily justice shirk!
"Apartheid," loudly let us cry
So that the world asks, "Israel, why?"

32. Resist Apartheid

Destruction is Israel's reply
    in an apartheid state.
Opponents have these rights—to die
    and be objects of hate.

The Palestinians are the ones
    that Israel wants to rout.
With bombs and automatic guns,
    it wants to get them out,

out of the so-called Holy Land
    by ev'ry evil means.
Let settlers with their weapons stand
    as perfect war machines.

In Israel is there surprise
    oppressed people resist?
One takes their land before their eyes;
    they've no means to exist.

Oppress a people year on year
    destroying life and land,
oppress them, making life so drear,
    they'll have to take a stand.

By drastic means they're justified
    to claim integrity.
There's such a thing as human pride
    to fight for equity.

"It is staggering how swiftly the ubiquitous negative stigma of 'antisemitism' is now applied on anybody who ethically and/or morally judges, critiques or condemns the state of Israel for its highly immoral, malevolent and vicious handling of the Palestinian people."[8]

33. The Antisemitic Stigma

It now's a negative stigma:
    the claim "You're Antisemitic!"
And yet it is an enigma
    why one cannot be a critic
of actions that are not moral,
    malicious, often violent.
With such actions one must quarrel,
    expose what is malevolent!

The UN brought to life a state,
    by "Israel" it now is known.
Its origin from unjust fate:
    the hatred Nazis Jews had shown.
The Nazis practiced genocide
    and confiscated homes and goods.
These injustices they amplified—
    destroying Jewish neighborhoods.

Ironically Israel now
    repeats this horrid history.
It does so with Nazi know-how
    through Palestinian misery.
It confiscates, destroys, and kills
    the Palestinian populus;
imprisons them as it so wills.
    Its actions are unscrupulous.

8. Charles Amjad-Ali, in his paper "Anti-Semitism—an Epithet to Shield Israel's Apartheid Practices."

The UN brought to life a state,
    by "Israel" now it is known,
but what of Palestinian fate?
    Is this state just for Jews alone?
Israeli settlements ignore
    the UN resolutions, laws,
Geneva Convention, and more—
    the State of Israel's laced with flaws.

"In arrogance the wicked pursue the poor—
let them be caught in the schemes they have devised.
For the wicked boast of the desires of their heart,
those greedy for gain curse and renounce the Lord."

34. Psalm 10:2–3

Some boast that they pursue the poor,
    for they are greedy for gain.
Rejection of the Lord is sure;
    they care not that they cause pain.

Their speech is filled with gross deceit;
    they catch the poor in their net:
ambush the helpless whom they cheat;
    to everyone they're a threat.

For justice now the psalmist prays,
    for God opposes deceit.
For justice let all voices raise,
    all greed and lust to defeat.

35. A Woman of Samaria[9]

A woman of Samaria
    knew prejudice firsthand,
hence when in her own area
    she heard a Jew's command:
"Give me to drink," he said that day,
    command or a request?
Help him or should she turn away?
    Was this some kind of test?

Jews with Samaritans refused
    to speak or fraternize;
she'd been rejected and abused
    before the village eyes.
She was surprised this Jew was kind
    and offered her a drink.
In "living water" would she find
    God's life-eternal link?

God's living water ever flows
    from springs of love divine.
Each one who drinks it quickly knows
    such love is yours and mine.
Samaritan, gentile, or Jew,
    we drink from the same well.
God's living love springs forth for you,
    for all who on earth dwell.

---

9. Read the story of the Samaritan woman and Jesus in John 4:4–42.

36. Persona non grata

In Israel, Christians, Muslims find
    they're citizens subclass.
Their ancestors are the wrong kind;
    they're written off *en masse.*

The slow and ruthless theft of land,
    with no place left to go,
shows clearly what is Israel's stand:
    persona non grata's so!

Persona non grata are words
    each Palestinian hears.
Oh my, did I forget the Kurds?
    They've heard these words for years.

37. Is Ethnic Cleansing a Defense?

Is ethnic cleansing a defense?
    Now Israel this view pursues.
"Let's drive the Palestinians hence,
    The path that Israel must choose!"

America, preach on, preach on
    about your democratic views,
such values all are long since gone,
    since you equality abuse.

The Zionists cry, "God sent us here,
    to claim the land as prophesied,"
as they in crystal balls now peer:
    they boldly justice set aside.

Fourteen hundred Israelis dead
    against thousands of Gazans killed.
Defense? Ethnic cleansing instead.
    Yet, violence has not violence stilled.

Speak out against madness of war,
    let Palestinians, Jews survive.
How can this be what life is for:
    let not a soul be left alive?

America, support just peace,
    America, heal lives of all.
America, war's funding cease,
    for US actions peace forestall.

SECTION 7
Justice

38. An Ancient Cry for Justice

The Hebrew prophets chose to speak
    against injustice, wrong,
for often wrong was at its peak,
    and evil deeds were strong.

To steal from others, they condemned,
    when wealthy wanted more,
and kings, from whom greed often stemmed,
    the prophets did deplore.

The prophet Amos pleads and pleads:
    let justice rush like streams[10]
of living water, meeting needs
    of those with justice dreams.

Isaiah says, "Learn to do good,
    seek justice for th' oppressed."[11]
And Jeremiah says you should
    "Seek justice, you'll be blessed."[12]

The prophet Micah spoke one day
    clearly, explicitly:
Do justice, love mercy, don't stray,
    walk in humility.[13]

Yes, justice, justice is the theme
    of Hebrew prophets' speech.
Who's willing this cause to redeem?
    Is it beyond all reach?

---

10. Amos 5:24.
11. Isaiah 1:17.
12. Jeremiah 22:3.
13. Micah 6:8.

Deuteronomy 16:19-20:
"You must not distort justice; you must not show partiality, and you must not accept bribes, for a bribe blinds the eyes of the wise and subverts the cause of those who are in the right. Justice, and only justice, you shall pursue, so that you may live and occupy the land that the Lord your God is giving you."

39. Do Not Pervert Justice

A sage of centuries ago
    recorded wise advice,
which some have chosen to forego
    at many a high price.

Accepted bribes at lives' expense,
    made rich the rich indeed;
they robbed the poor without pretense,
    and cared not what they need.

Perverting justice blinds the eyes,
    subverts the righteous' cause;
it robs the wisdom of the wise,
    and violates God's laws.

The unjust forfeit what's to come,
    inheritance is lost.
Their lives are mis'rable and glum;
    for they ignored the cost.

40. Justice, Justice Plead!

In Israel, Gaza, Palestine
 will no one "justice" heed,
a land with justice in decline—
 its people justice plead!

41. Justice, Justice Is the Cry

The Hebrew prophets did arise
    with messages of justice, turn.
"From evil, turn," was no surprise
    for Israel did God's justice spurn.

A single prophet's loud outcry?
    No, hosts of them kept speaking out.
Hear now the widows', children's sigh:
    "You starve the poor, there is no doubt."

"You steal our land, what shall we do?"
    asks Amos in a pow'rful voice.
"Do justice," cries the Psalmist[14] too,
    for justice only is God's choice.

Does this sound like the ancient past,
    or something one hears still today?
The prophets' cry will last and last:
    injustices on humans prey!

So Israel's prophets must be heard,
    they offer hope to humankind.
But only if we prize this word:
    "Keep justice, justice on your mind."

---

14. Psalms 33:5, 140:12.

42. Equality and Justice for All

To segregate and isolate
    after the Civil War
became the way to legislate,
    create the cultural core
of many of the southern states
    for decades yet to come,
where racism perpetrates
    life that proceeds therefrom.

The movement known as Civil Rights
    brought progress, to be sure,
but many still defend the whites
    and want no cultural cure.
Still there are those who justice prize,
    fight for equality,
while others simply close their eyes,
    lapse into lethargy.

The US claims "justice for all,"
    ignores it yet at will.
Indeed, this is its great downfall
    and does so with great skill.
In Israel apartheid reigns
    or segregation plus,
for Palestinians "live in chains."
    Their rights?—do not discuss!

Our US government supports
    Israel every year
with billions in aid per reports,
    though rights just disappear.
Though segregation we oppose
    at home, why not abroad?
Democracy is Israel's pose,
    but is it there a fraud?

Apartheid and segregation
    are basically the same.
The new name a "Jewish Nation"
    excludes non-Jews by name,
especially Palestinian—
    no human rights, no land.
Whatever your opinion,
    for justice take a stand!

One cannot Hamas' terror bless,
    though occupation primed.
More violence is an abscess—
    for peace efforts ill-timed.
Fight violence with violence
    the usual human way,
but violence has no recompense
    except with death to pay.

America, hypocrisy
    is written on your face,
for to the term "democracy"
    your actions bring disgrace.
Apartheid or segregation
    oppose, yes, in your land,
but do not support a nation
    that will not take this stand!

SECTION 8
Grace

43. Never Again #2

It's time to say, "Never again,"
    "Never again will there be war!"
Never again endure the pain,
    never attracted by the lore
that by the choice of God on high
    some rights may have and others none.
There are the chosen few whereby
    the promised land's forever won.

To victors always go the spoils,
    we've heard from ancient ages past,
but such a view often embroils
    all those who've been displaced, outcast.
Where does this still take place today?
    "America and Palestine,
Iraq, Afghanistan," you say.
    There voices loudly shout, "That's mine!"

The colonializing voices cry,
    consistently, "That's mine, that's mine!"
It matters not who'll have to die:
    the victor's rights are rights divine.
Today some Christians and some Jews
    avow God promised Jews the land.
In Palestine God will suffuse
    the chosen people, as God planned.

How can it be a God of love
>would choose some people to abuse,
while placing others far above
>all justice; does not this confuse
the Bible's claim that "God is love,"[15]
>the nature of almighty God?
If we cannot partake thereof,
>then Jews and Christians are a fraud.

---

15. 1 John 4:8.

44. Weaponizing the Bible

Held high the Bible's long discourse
has made it centuries-long a force
for actions of morality
and actions of mortality.
Some weaponize the Bible's texts
and think they know what God expects.
The texts they gladly weaponize
to give them rights to colonize.

This happens in the Holy Land
where Palestinians now are banned
from taking recourse to reclaim
land, houses, since they are to blame:
they are the strangers with no rights,
outcasts just like the Edomites.
To colonize is justified,
for history is Israel's guide.

America, England, and France
to native peoples gave no chance.
They colonized, took native land,
bold ethnic cleansing then they planned.
Should not then Israel follow suit:
convict and kill without dispute?
Does Scripture say, God chose the Jews,
so they may all non-Jews abuse?

Do you think God discriminates,
assigns some higher, lower fates?
The Scriptures say that "God is love,"[16]
and God's New Israel's above

---

16. 1 John 4:8.

land theft and murder of God's own,
for God would leave no one alone.
In Christ, God love personifies;
a love for all that never dies.

45. Grace

Is grace something that one can learn?
    Is grace something that can be taught?
Can grace be found where'er you turn?
    Is grace something that's better caught?

Grace is not something you possess,
    yet grace is something you can give.
Grace finds unusual ways to bless,
    and grace is the best way to live.

You'll find that grace you cannot earn,
    and it's not something you can win.
But grace in others you'll discern;
    they'll know if you with grace begin.

Where is it that one may find grace?—
    a loving hand, a tender smile,
a kind deed and a warm embrace,
    someone who goes the second mile.

God's grace is all of this and more,
    encompassing the universe.
It has unceasing love in store;
    love can the power of hate reverse.

46. Forgiveness

Have we forgotten to forgive?
Without forgiveness can we live?
Without it, what have we to give?

Forgiveness needs humility
which nurtures the ability
to care with sensibility.

Forgiveness means caring concern
for self and others to discern.
Can we, each one, forgiveness learn?

Forgiveness is not a born trait;
for many it comes much too late,
yet it can overcome one's hate.

Forgiveness, posture all supreme,
can life from its worst qualms redeem.
Forgiveness should be our life's theme.

47. The Art of Forgiveness

Forgiveness is a long, lost art,
for it requires an open heart.
It waits not for apology;
it's not tied to chronology.
It is the posture of the heart;
is unaware that it is smart.
Forgiveness can heal angry souls
when tension seems beyond controls.
Forgiveness has the power to heal;
it's something you can truly feel.
Forgiveness does not mean you're weak,
but reconciliation seek.
If you have ever been forgiven,
you have a brief foretaste of heaven.

48. Love One's Enemy! Insane!

War's never patient, never kind;
war's always thoughtless, always blind.
War parties claim that they're for peace,
but on their terms or war won't cease.
For vengeance wants to have its way:
opponents with their lives must pay.
Revenge creates the sacrifice
of moral will at any price.
Revenge and vengeance are strong willed;
with hatred inhumane they're filled.
Revenge cares not for parent, child,
for war revenge is aptly styled:
it kills the living in its path,
each soul a victim of war's wrath.
Some scoff at Jesus' simple way
to care for others, come what may.
"To love an enemy's insane,"
say those who Jesus' way disdain.
To those who simply can't decide
the world awaits this to be tried.

49. Humane

Humane's a word often ignored,
but can we humans this afford?
If humans cannot be humane,
then life itself they will profane,
for no compassion will be shown,
benevolence will not be known.
Humane is a compelling word;
without it, life will be absurd.
Never to hear said, "Be humane,"
makes life each day surely inane.
Humane, source of civility,
humane's what everyone should be.

50. To Conquer

Why "conquer" is a constant word
    we read in history.
Why leaders often it preferred
    remains no mystery.

"To conquer" means you win the day,
    be it for good or bad.
It means somehow you've had your way,
    a reason to be glad?

One thinks of conquering leaders like
    Attila, Genghis Khan,
who conquered with each deadly strike
    at evening or at dawn.

But one can conquer differently
    with words and devious ways,
and not coincidentally
    it's dignity one slays.

What if all conquering were for grace
    and human dignity?
The world would be a better place,
    full of felicity!

Bibliography

Amjad-Ali, Charles. "Prejudice and Its Historical Application: A Radical Hermeneutic of Luther's Treatment of the Turks (Muslims) and the Jews," in Ulrich Duchrow and Craig Nessan, eds., *Radicalizing Reformation Volume 4: Liberation from Violence for Life in Peace.* Berlin, Germany: LIT Verlag Dr. Hopf, 2015, 105-42.

Dawidowicz, Lucy. *The War Against the Jews, 1933-1945.* New York: Holt, Rinehart and Winston, 1975, xxi-xxiii.

Goldhagen, Daniel Jonah. *Hitler's Willing Executioners: Ordinary Germans and the Holocaust.* New York: Vintage, 1997.

———. *A Moral Reckoning: the Role of the Catholic Church in the Holocaust and its Unfulfilled Duty of Repair.* New York: Vintage Books, 2002.

Kimbrough, S T, Jr. *Who Cares About the Middle East? Poems for Reflection and Conviction.* Eugene, OR: Wipf and Stock, 2021.

———. *Why Should a Child Be Born? Poems for Peace and Justice in the Middle East.* Eugene, OR: Wipf and Stock, 2018.

Kipling, Rudyard, "White Man's Burden: The United States & the Philippine Islands, 1899." First published in the February 1899 issue of *McClure's Magazine*, and later in *Rudyard Kipling's Verse: Definitive Edition.* Garden City, NJ: Doubleday, 1929.

Marx, Karl. "On the Jewish Question" in *Deutsch-Französische Jahrbücher.* February, 1844.

Orwell, George. *Animal Farm.* London: Secker and Warburg, 1945.

Index of Biblical References

The page numbers are followed by numbers of the respective poems (within parentheses) to which the biblical references are related.

Genesis
1:26–27　　　　　x

Leviticus
11:44　　　x, 35 (#22)
19:18　　　x, 43 (#27)

Deuteronomy
16:19–20　　x, 60 (#39)

Psalms
4:4　　　　x, 18 (#12)
10:2–3　　x, 53 (#34)
33:5　　　x, 62 (#41)
140:12　　x, 62 (#41)

Isaiah
1:17　　　　　　x, xxvi,
　　　　33 (#21), 59 (#38)

Jeremiah
22:3　　　　　　x, xxvi,
　　　　　　　　59 (#38)

Amos
5:24　　　　　59 (#38)

Micah
6:8　　　　x, 59 (#38)

Matthew
5:44　　　　　　xxix

John
4:4–42　　x, 54 (#35)

Acts
2:17–18　　　　　x

2 Corinthians
5:19–20　　　　　x

Ephesians
4:26　　　x, 18 (#12)

1 John
4:8　　　　x, xi, xxviii,
　　　　68 (#43), 69 (#44)

www.ingramcontent.com/pod-product-compliance
Lightning Source LLC
Chambersburg PA
CBHW061452040426
42450CB00007B/1328